PRICE
10
CENTS

A WONDERFUL
COLLECTION OF HARDY AND HALF HARDY
CLIMBERS

PEAS

"The kingdom of Heaven is like a mustard seed."
Matthew 13:31
NIV

A WONDERFUL COLLECTION of HARDY and HALF HARDY

CLIMBERS

PEAS

Christie Jones Ray

°°Goats Milk

and Gardening°°

© Copyright 2012

ISBN 978-0-9853223-9-7

Rose Water Cottage Press

PRICE
10
CENTS

A WONDERFUL COLLECTION of HARDY and HALF HARDY

CLIMBERS

PEAS

This little book is
dedicated to the extraordinary
students at Orlando Junior Academy
for the garden they made . . .
under the gentle guidance of
Mr. Brad Jones

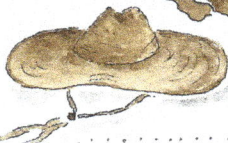

A WONDERFUL
COLLECTION OF HARDY AND HALF HARDY

CLIMBERS

PEAS

Goat's milk and gardening ... What do you think?

The Private World of Tasha Tudor   Tudor an

PRICE
10
CENTS

A WONDERFUL COLLECTION OF HARDY AND HALF HARDY

CLIMBERS

◆ PEAS ◆

I heard
from an old friend...
and yes... it is true.
Narry a headache,
if this
you will do.

A WONDERFUL
COLLECTION OF HARDY AND HALF HARDY

CLIMBERS

PEAS

Each day
as you rise...
and breakfast
you make ...

A WONDERFUL
COLLECTION OF HARDY AND HALF HARDY

CLIMBERS

PEAS

Reach
for the goat's milk,
and fill up your glass.

GOAT'S
Milk

PRICE
10
CENTS

A WONDERFUL COLLECTION OF HARDY AND HALF HARDY

CLIMBERS

PEAS

Then walk
to the garden
with trowel and rake.

A WONDERFUL
COLLECTION OF HARDY AND HALF HARDY
CLIMBERS

✦ PEAS ✦

Breathe in
the fresh air
and straighten
your hat.

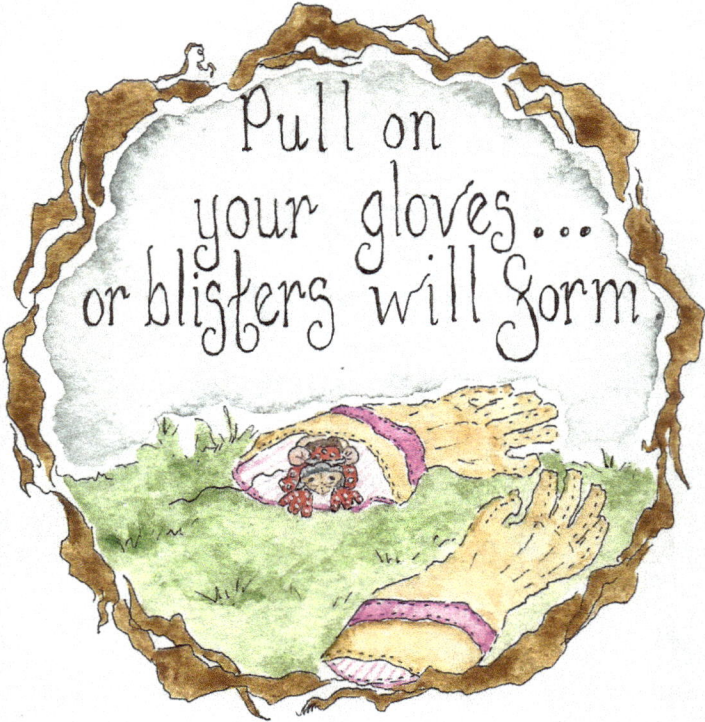

A WONDERFUL
COLLECTION OF HARDY AND HALF HARDY

CLIMBERS

• PEAS •

Drop in
each seed . . .
with a wish and
a prayer.

A WONDERFUL
COLLECTION of HARDY and HALF HARDY

CLIMBERS

❧ PEAS ❧

...and pat
down the dirt with
love and with care.

Pat Pat Pat Pat Pat

A WONDERFUL
COLLECTION of HARDY and HALF HARDY

CLIMBERS

•PEAS•

Prayers...
for more sunshine...
more wind ...
and more rain.

A WONDERFUL COLLECTION OF HARDY AND HALF HARDY CLIMBERS

PEAS

Just
when you think ...
... you can't wait
much longer ...

Garden
10:00

PRICE
10
CENTS

A WONDERFUL
COLLECTION OF HARDY AND HALF HARDY

CLIMBERS

PEAS

...a green
little sprout looks
up
as it's yawning.

A WONDERFUL
COLLECTION of HARDY and HALF HARDY

CLIMBERS

❧ **PEAS** ❧

Hello,
little Sprout,
you say as you wonder...

PRICE
10
CENTS

A WONDERFUL
COLLECTION of HARDY and HALF HARDY

CLIMBERS

PEAS

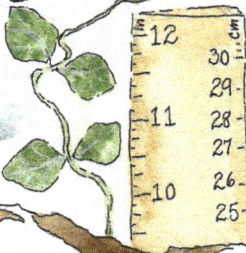

how tall
it will grow
and where
it will spiral.

A WONDERFUL COLLECTION OF HARDY AND HALF HARDY CLIMBERS

PEAS

Up
to the top
of a trellis
or twig...

A WONDERFUL COLLECTION of HARDY and HALF HARDY

CLIMBERS

·PEAS·

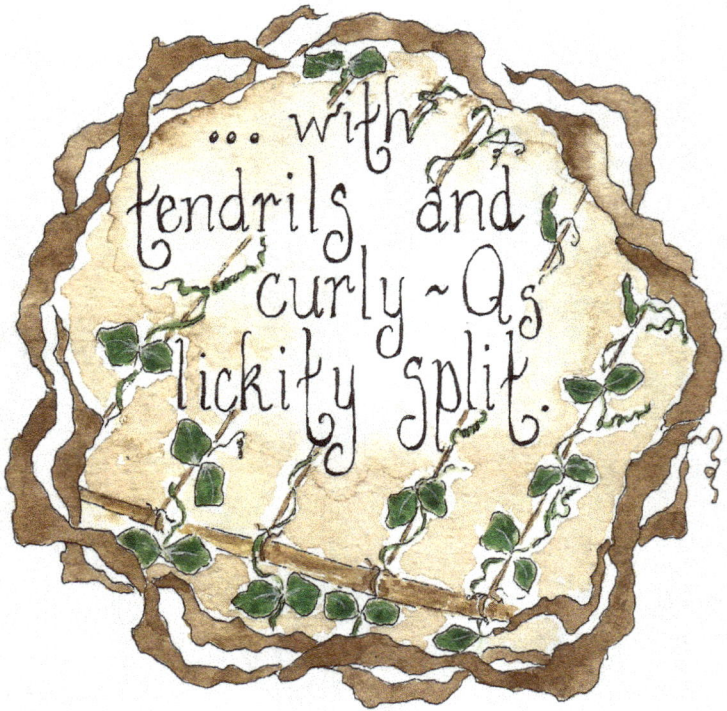

... with
tendrils and
curly ~ Qs
lickity split.

A WONDERFUL
COLLECTION OF HARDY AND HALF HARDY
CLIMBERS

PEAS

English
or
Sugar Snaps...
which one is which?

A WONDERFUL
COLLECTION OF HARDY AND HALF HARDY
CLIMBERS
PEAS

Each
has a pod
like a tiny
green ship.

S.S. Pea Pod

A WONDERFUL COLLECTION OF HARDY AND HALF HARDY

CLIMBERS

PEAS

English
pea pods
have a string
like a zipper.

A WONDERFUL
COLLECTION of HARDY and HALF HARDY

CLIMBERS

PEAS

Sugar Snap
pea pods
stay closed
till they're eaten.

PRICE
10
CENTS

A WONDERFUL
COLLECTION OF HARDY AND HALF HARDY

CLIMBERS

PEAS

Those are the ones you can pick off the vine.

A WONDERFUL
COLLECTION of HARDY and HALF HARDY

CLIMBERS
•PEAS•

They are
sweet and quite
crunchy...
just as they
ripen.

A WONDERFUL COLLECTION of HARDY and HALF HARDY

CLIMBERS

PEAS

Never
devour
the pod
of the other...

A WONDERFUL
COLLECTION OF HARDY AND HALF HARDY
CLIMBERS

PEAS

...but
open it gently...
and there you'll
discover...

A WONDERFUL
COLLECTION OF HARDY AND HALF HARDY

CLIMBERS

PEAS

Round
little peas ... so
green and so
pretty...

A WONDERFUL COLLECTION OF HARDY AND HALF HARDY  CLIMBERS

PEAS

waiting to roll on your plate and be eaten.

PRICE
10
CENTS

A WONDERFUL COLLECTION OF HARDY AND HALF HARDY

CLIMBERS

PEAS

Don't you
feel clever . . .
. . . so smart
and so proud ?

PRICE **10** CENTS

A WONDERFUL COLLECTION OF HARDY AND HALF HARDY

CLIMBERS

•PEAS•

You've planted... and tended... and gathered... and prepped.

A WONDERFUL
COLLECTION OF HARDY AND HALF HARDY

CLIMBERS

PEAS

Ask now, for God's blessing... and never forget...

A WONDERFUL COLLECTION OF HARDY AND HALF HARDY

CLIMBERS

PEAS

He brings the sunshine, the wind, and the rain.

A WONDERFUL COLLECTION OF HARDY AND HALF HARDY  CLIMBERS

PEAS

Goat's milk
and gardening...
What do you think?

A WONDERFUL
COLLECTION OF HARDY AND HALF HARDY

CLIMBERS

❧ **PEAS** ❧

I think she was
wise...
that old friend
of mine.

PRICE
10
CENTS

A WONDERFUL
COLLECTION OF HARDY AND HALF HARDY
CLIMBERS

◆ PEAS ◆

Drink
all your
goat's milk
when starting
your day...

www.ingramcontent.com/pod-product-compliance
Lightning Source LLC
Chambersburg PA
CBHW072056040426
42447CB00012BB/3146